Introducing
THE
HIGHLANDS
OF SCOTLAND

A D Cameron

**with photography by
Dennis Hardley &
Andrew McKenna**

*the land
and the people*

To the Orkney Islands · *Duncet Head* · To the Orkney Islands
Cape Wrath
Strathy Point · Scrabster · *Duncansby Head* · John o'Groats
Durness · Dunnet · Castletown
Talmine · Tongue · **Bettyhill** · Melvich · Reay · **Thurso** · Halkirk · Keiss
Kinlochbervie · Armadale · *Loch Hope* · Ben Hope 927 · *Loch Loyal* · Forsinard · Watten · **Wick**
Rhiconich · Foinaven 908 · *C a i t h n e s s* · A9
Handa · Arkle 786 · Achfary · Altnaharra · Ben Klibreck 721 · Kinbrace · Dunbeath
Scourie · *S u t h e r l a n d* · Morven 705
Point of Stoer · Drumbeg · Kylesku · *Loch Naver* · *Strath of Kildonan* · Berriedale
Stoer · *Loch Shin* · Overscaig · **Helmsdale**
Loch Assynt · Ben More Assynt 998 · Brora
Lochinver · Suilven 731 · Lairg · Rogart · Golspie
Elphin · *Strath Brora* · Embo
Summer Isles · Achiltibuie · Rosehall · Invershin · **Dornoch**
To the Western Isles · *Strath Oykel* · Bonar Bridge · Ardgay · *Tarbat Ness* · Portmahomack
Ullapool · Carn Ban 842 · *C r o m a r t y* · Tain
Badluarach · Beinn Dearg 1081 · Ardross · Balintore
Aultbea · Dundonnell · Ardross · Nigg · *Moray Firth* · Findhorn
Poolewe · An Teallach 1062 · Ben Wyvis 1046 · Evanton · Cromarty
Gairloch · *R o s s a n d* · Sgurr Mor 1109 · Dingwall · Fortrose · **Nairn** · Forres · To Aberdeen
Badachro · Slioch 981 · Kinlochewe · **Strathpeffer** · Auldearn
Diabaig · Beinn Alligin 985 · Beinn Eighe 972 · Achnasheen · *Strath Conon* · Muir of Ord · North **Kessock** · Cawdor · Croy
Torridon · Liathach 1054 · Shieldaig · *I n v e r n e s s* · Beauly · **Inverness** · Ferness
Applecross · Glen Carron · Sgurr a'Chaorachain 1053 · Loch Monar · Struy · Kiltarlity · Davvot
Lochcarron · Strathcarron · Sgurr na Lapaich 1150 · Carnoch · Drumnadrochit · *Grantown on Spey*
Kishorn · *Glen Strathfarrar* · Cannich · Tomich · Dulnain Bridge
Plockton · *Loch Mullardoch* · Carrbridge · Nethy Bridge
Stromeferry · Dornie · Carn Eighe 1182 · Tomatin · Boat of Garten · To Tomintoul
Kyle of Lochalsh · Balmacara · *Glen Urquhart* · Fayers · Glenmore
Kyleakin · **Shiel Bridge** · The Five Sisters · Cluanie · Whitebridge · **Aviemore**
Kylerhea · *Glen Shiel* · Invermoriston · Kincraig · Feshiebridge · *C a i r n g o r m*
Broadford · Arnisdale · Kinlochourn · **Fort Augustus** · *Mountains* · Ben Macdui 1309
S k y e · Glenbrittle · Cuillin Hills · Ladhar Bheinn 1019 · *Knoydart* · Sgurr Mor 1003 · South Laggan · Newtonmore · **Kingussie**
Elgol · Ord · Sron a'Choire Ghairbh 935 · Laggan Bridge · *S t r a t h s p e y*
Mallaig · Ardvasar · Armadale · Invergarry · *Loch Oich* · Dalwhinnie
Morar · Invarie · Letterfinlay · Creag Meagaidh 1128 · *C a n n a*
Rum · *Loch Morar* · Sgurr Thuilm 964 · Gairlochy · Roy Bridge · To Perth and Edinburgh
Eigg · Arisaig · Sgurr Arkaig · Ben Alder 1148 · Chno Dearg 1046
Port Mor · Lochailort · Glenfinnan · Kinlocheil · Corpach · **Spean Bridge**
Muck · Glenuig · *Moidart* · Meall Mor 758 · Ben Nevis 1344 · *Loch Treig*
Kinlochmoidart · Acharacle · Sgurr Dhomhnuill 888 · **Fort William** · Mamores · *Rannoch Moor*
Ardnamurchan Point · Salen · Ardgour · Corran · Kinlochleven
To the Western Isles · Kilchoan · Glenborrodale · **Strontian** · Beinn nam 1145 · To Perth and Edinburgh
To Coll and Tiree · Drimnin · CreachBheinn 853 · **Ballachulish** · Glencoe · *Glen Coe*
M o r v e n · Kingairloch · Duror · *Rannoch Moor*
Tobermory · Port Appin · *Loch Etive*
Kilchoan · Lochaline · To Oban · To Crianlarich and Glasgow
Mull · To Oban

Tourist Infomation Offices
open all year
seasonal
Railway line
A roads
B and other roads
National Tourist Route
Ferries
vehicle
passenger

0   20 miles
0   20 Kilometres

Welcome to the Highlands, all the north and west which makes up half the total area of Scotland. This is a land of mountains and lochs, of rock and peat, of moorland and pasture, its arable land limited to the north-east coast and the mouths of the glens.

Approaching from the fertile Lowlands to the south, the mountain peaks appear in the distance and, about thirty kilometres north of Glasgow, Stirling and Perth, they give the Highlands a sharply defined edge. This is known as *The Highland Line* or *The Highland Boundary Fault*. It turns north to exclude the rich farmland of Kincardineshire and Aberdeenshire, and then north-west towards Inverness.

The mountains in the Highlands are not very high compared with mountain ranges elsewhere, such as the Alps. Mont Blanc (4807m), for example, is more than three times the height of Ben Nevis (1343m or 4406feet), which is Scotland's, and Britain's, highest mountain. Among hill-walkers in Britain peaks above 3000 feet (or 914 metres) are recognised as mountains, now called *Munros*, after Hugh T Munro who listed them over a century ago. In Scotland there are 277, all in the Highlands; in Wales there may be 8 but those who have climbed them say 14; in England there are 4, in the Lake District; and in Ireland 8. The presence of so many mountains and hills is the chief attraction of the Highlands within the British Isles. Their awesome presence and their closeness to water - loch or waterfall, sparkling stream or the sea - are the elements of scenery of infinite variety under an ever changing sky.

Of the Highland landscape Sir Walter Scott's words ring true:

O, Caledonia! stern and wild
Meet nurse for a poetic child
Land of brown heath and
shaggy wood
Land of the mountain and
the flood
Land of my sires!...

The Making of the Mountains

About 400 million years ago - so long ago that it is impossible to imagine - an era of tumultuous change began as huge areas of the earth's crust were torn apart. The Caledonian mountains were thrust upwards to a height far higher than today and in one of the cracks or faults running from SW to NE from Loch Linnhe to the Moray Firth, the Great Glen was created, effectively cutting the Highlands into two parts. Among the outstanding mountains, the Cairngorms and Ben Nevis consist of granite, except for Ben Nevis' basalt top,

GLEN ROY NATIONAL NATURE RESERVE

HOW THE PARALLEL ROADS WERE FORMED

PLEASE KEEP DOGS ON A LEAD : FOLLOW THE COUNTRY CODE

while Suilven and Quinag, mountains in the north-west with shapes and personalities of their own, Quinag with a top of Cambrian quartzite, are of Torridonian sandstone, like the mountains of Torridon themselves. Created much later, about 60 million years ago, the Black Cuillins in Skye are made of rough and hard volcanic rock, known as gabbro.

Changes to a much colder world climate caused the Highlands to be completely covered in ice, as much as 5000 feet thick during a long series of ice ages, the last of which ended only 10,000 years ago. Glaciers pick up rocks underneath them and as they moved, they ground down the sides of mountains to create U-shaped valleys and scooped out huge corries and vast hollows which on ice-melt became deep lochs such as Loch Ness and Loch Morar.

The Parallel Roads of Glen Roy, which are not 'roads' but shore lines of a loch blocked by ice at different stages, provide vivid proof that the melting of the ice was a long and slow process. Relieved of the burden of the ice, the Highlands rose up

Opposite: *The parallel roads in Glen Roy, evidence of successive shore lines as the last Ice Age ended.*

clear of the sea, with raised beaches and sheer cliffs in places facing the sea. With warmer weather plants and trees began to grow and animals began to move in.

The First Highlanders

Mountainous areas are never easy places to make a living but on the water's edge people could collect shell-fish and catch fish. Pointed implements and knives of flint found on the shore of Loch Torridon and of bloodstone on Rum are clues left by the earliest people.

The more fertile north-east attracted farmers, keeping

Above: *The scattered houses of Torridon, typical of many coastal settlements in the Highlands.*

cattle and sheep, clearing the forest and growing crops such as barley. Their settlements on the mainland await discovery, unlike Orkney, but their chambered tombs are evidence of their numbers and the power of the men who organised the labour and the engineering skills to construct them in the 4th and 3rd millennia BC. In Caithness Camster Round, which can still be entered, has a corbelled roof, while Camster Long beside it is 70 metres long. Near Inverness are the Clava Cairns, three round

tombs in a row, two with passages along which the setting sun would have shone into the tombs on midwinter's day. Rings of tall standing stones surround each tomb. Clava today has the atmosphere of a place set apart, a place where people assembled for religious ritual and ceremony.

Wetter, colder weather, setting in about 1000 BC and continuing, led to a blanket of peat (later to be fuel for the Highlanders) being laid down, sometimes over land which had been cultivated. Quarrels over land, and probably also the growth of tribal organisation saw people building forts with high stone walls, or stone and timber walls, on the tops of hills as places to be safe in. Craig Phadrig near Inverness, built about 400 BC is a good example of the second type. Still occupied a thousand years later, Craig Phadrig may also have been the capital of Brudei, a king of the Picts whom St Columba visited near the River Ness.

The commonest defensive structure in the north and west

Opposite: *The shore of Loch Torridon and a view of Beinn Alligin, Wester Ross.*

Right: *Dun Telve, near Glenelg, west Inverness-shire, the best preserved broch on the Scottish mainland.*

Photo: A D Cameron

Photo: Dennis Hardley

is the *broch*, which is found in no other country in Europe. It is a great round tower with double walls of stone, open at the top but with no openings on the outside, except for a low entrance which could be blocked by a stone door. Impossible to climb, it was a place to live safely inside. The best preserved examples are Dun Telve (still

Opposite: *In contrast to the mountainous, rugged north and west, this pastoral scene near Contin is typical of the gentler landscape in the east.* Photo: Dennis Hardley

Above: *The rich, fertile land of the Black Isle north of Inverness benefits from a drier, sunnier climate than the west.*

over 10 metres high) and Dun Troddan, near Glenelg.

Picts, Scots and Vikings.

In 297 AD the Romans, who failed to conquer the Highlands, described the Caledonians and other tribesmen attacking Roman Britain as *Picti*, 'the painted men'. They were not a new people but a new name for all the Highland people until the

Scots from Ireland invaded Argyll in the 5th and 6th centuries AD. *Gaelic*, the language the invading Scots spoke, spread until it became the language of all Highland people and their name, Scots, came to cover all the people in the much enlarged country of Scotland.

From Ireland too came St Columba in 563 AD with twelve companions and made the island of Iona a religious centre from which to take the story of Christ to the Scots and the Picts.

Proof of their success can be seen in the fine Christian crosses on stone slabs by Pictish sculptors far from Iona at Rosemarkie, Nigg and Shandwick in Easter Ross.

The *Vikings* from Scandinavia came first as raiders, then from about the year 800 as settlers in the Northern and Western Isles and on the mainland in Caithness, Wester Ross and Sutherland, which to their earls in Orkney meant 'southern land'. By 900 AD they too had become Christian.

In the Middle Ages

It was difficult for Scottish kings in the south to control the Highlands. David I (1124-53) and his successors introduced Norman feudal lords to act for them. Inverness at the mouth of the Great Glen soon had a royal castle with a sheriff to represent royal authority. Thomas Durward, sheriff of Inverness, on gaining the lands of Urquhart in 1229, chose a commanding position on Loch Ness to build Urquhart Castle. The Comyns, later to be rivals of Robert the

Above: *Urquhart Castle by Loch Ness now in the care of Historic Scotland and being visited by 200,000 people a year*

Bruce, built Inverlochy Castle to dominate the south-west end of the Great Glen. Many Highlanders fought for Bruce, King Robert I, including Stewarts, Mackintoshes, Campbells and some MacDonalds, securing Scotland's independence from England at the Battle of Bannockburn on 1314.

Earlier, in the twelfth century, Somerled a chief in the west who had a ship conquered the islands and claimed to be 'King of the Isles'. Descendants of his took the title 'Lord of the Isles', one leading an army away to the east to fight the Battle of Harlaw (1411) near Aberdeen, another

burning Inverness and being imprisoned by James I. Not till 1493 did James IV end the challenge of the Lord of the Isles to his own authority. The price he paid, however, was that he removed the one person with the power locally to keep the Highland chiefs in order. Soon they began to behave as if they were kings as well.

Clans and Chiefs

The word *clan* means 'the children' and the chief was like an all-powerful father to them.

He was not, of course, the real father of all of them. His relatives, who had the clan surname, held land directly from him and they were the clan's prime fighting men. The lands where each clan lived are shown on the map on page 16. People with other surnames who lived there were also members of the clan.

Within this clan structure Gaelic culture reached its height, much of it in the oral tradition - the telling and re-telling of stories remembered about earlier times and the telling of new ones about clan heroes and characters, the making of poetry, the singing of songs either to entertain at a *ceilidh*, or gathering, or else to accompany work. At the same time *pibroch*, the classical bagpipe music was developed, especially by the MacCrimmon family in Skye. In the seventeenth century a chief would usually have his own piper, many of whom had been trained by the MacCrimmons.

Opposite: *A feature of a Highland summer evening is the afterglow which lingers after the sun has set in the west. Here the Cuillins of Skye stand silhouetted in the evening light.*

Right: *A piper plays the pibroch at Glenfinnan whilst experienced ears listen to every note.*

A chief could judge his clansmen in his court and had the right even to hang them. Also their commander in battle, he could call them to war by sending round the fiery cross, charred by fire and smeared with blood. Often this was for a clan feud: the MacDonells of Glengarry often feuded with the Mackenzies, for example. It might be taking sides in a war, Clan Donald supporting the Marquis of Montrose in his year of victories (1644-5) in the Civil War, and many clans fighting under 'Bonnie Dundee' at Killiecrankie (1689) on behalf of Catholic James VII and II against Dutch William III's army. The stray bullet which killed Dundee took the edge off their victory. The treatment Government troops meted out to one small clan, the MacDonalds of Glencoe, in 1692 after enjoying their hospitality in their homes for nearly a fortnight, by putting 38 of them to the sword is ever remembered as 'the Massacre of Glencoe'.

Opposite: *The Pass of Glencoe not far from the place where MacDonalds of Glencoe were slaughtered in 1692.*

Right: *Glenshiel near 'Spaniards' Pass' where a small Jacobite army with Spanish support was defeated in 1719. Interestingly, solitary rowans are a feature of both landscapes.*

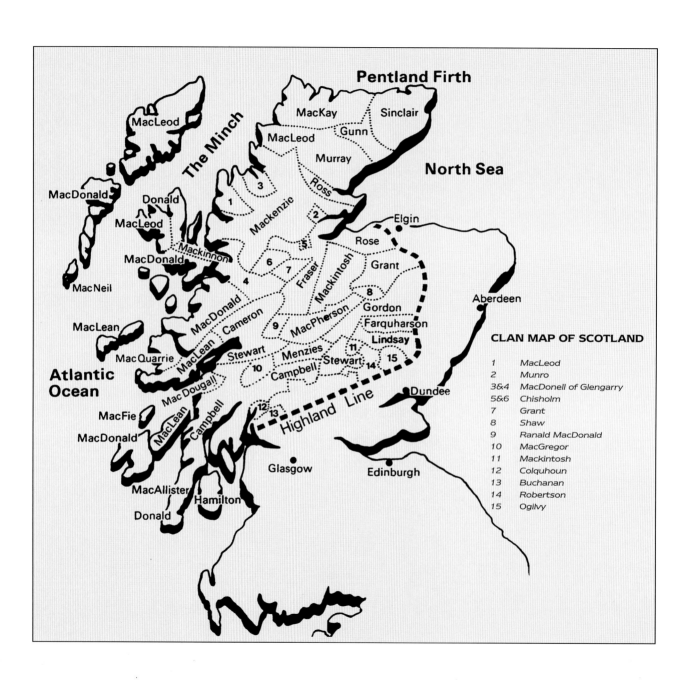

Pentland Firth

MacLeod

The Minch

MacKay

Sinclair

Gunn

MacLeod

Murray

North Sea

MacDonald

Donald

3

1

Ross

MacLeod

Mackenzie

2

MacKinnon

5

Rose

Elgin

MacDonald

6

7

Fraser

Mackintosh

Grant

MacNeil

4

Aberdeen

8

Atlantic
Ocean

MacLean

MacDonald

9

MacPherson

Gordon

MacQuarrie

MacLean

Cameron

Farquharson

Lindsay

MacLean

Stewart

Menzies

Stewart

14

15

11

Campbell

MacDougall

10

13

Dundee

MacFie

12

Highland Line

MacDonald

MacLean

Campbell

Glasgow

Edinburgh

MacAllister

Hamilton

Donald

CLAN MAP OF SCOTLAND

1	*MacLeod*
2	*Munro*
3&4	*MacDonell of Glengarry*
5&6	*Chisholm*
7	*Grant*
8	*Shaw*
9	*Ranald MacDonald*
10	*MacGregor*
11	*Mackintosh*
12	*Colquhoun*
13	*Buchanan*
14	*Robertson*
15	*Ogilvy*

Photo: Dennis Hardley

Jacobite Risings

By 1714 when George of Hanover became King George I of Great Britain, no one else except Highland chiefs could raise armies of fighting men. Some rose as *Jacobites*, 'followers of James', son of James VII, a Catholic who claimed to be king. Their rising in 1715 ended in a drawn battle at Sheriffmuir near Stirling. Another

in 1719 with the aid of 300 Spanish troops ended in defeat in what is still called 'Spaniards' Pass' in Glenshiel.

After this the Government stationed Redcoats in forts along the Great Glen, Fort William, Fort Augustus and Fort George in Inverness. General George Wade used his own soldiers to construct roads to allow troops to move easily

Above: *A section of Fort George, built east of Inverness after the 'Forty five, the finest Hanoverian fort in Britain.*

between forts and also to connect them with the Lowlands. This was the first important step towards opening up the Highlands:

> *If you had seen these roads before they were made,*
> *You'd hold up your hands and bless General Wade.*

Eilean Donan Castle on Loch Duich.

Much later, in 1745, when Prince Charles Edward, 'Bonnie Prince Charlie', grandson of James VII, landed in the west with only seven followers, many Highland chiefs refused to join him. MacDonalds and Camerons, however, raised the standard of rebellion at Glenfinnan and swept south, gathering support on the way. They captured Edinburgh and marched as far south as Derby, only 120 miles from London. Gaining no support in England they turned and conducted a heroic retreat back to the Highlands, with Government forces on their heels. At Culloden near Inverness on 16 April 1746 their weary army of clansmen was overwhelmed by the cannon and bayonets of the British Army. This turned out to be the last battle fought on British soil.

Decline of the Clans
Redcoats devastated the Jacobite glens with fire and sword and stayed on in the forts as an army of occupation.

New laws prevented Highlanders from possessing weapons, wearing the kilt or any garment of tartan or even playing

Opposite: The pipes and drums of The Queens Own Highlanders (Seaforth and Camerons) march on the Parade, Fort William.

Above: *Loch Stack and Ben Arkle in Sutherland.*

the bagpipes, which were deemed to be 'instruments of war'.

Jacobite chiefs lost their lands and all chiefs lost the right to judge their men. No longer military leaders, no longer judges, clan chiefs became like any other landlords, treating the clan lands as their own, and clanship continued to decay.

Before the 'Forty-five the first Highland regiment, the Black Watch, had been raised to prevent cattle-stealing. After it several regiments of Highlanders were raised to fight *for* the Government - the Seaforth Highlanders, the Cameron Highlanders and the Sutherland Highlanders, for example. They

continued to wear the kilt of their own distinctive tartan and their bands of pipers and drummers became part of the tradition of the Highland regiments in the British Army.

Cattle, Sheep and Deer
Keeping cattle, which provided milk, butter and cheese, and growing oats and barley on narrow strips of land, cultivated by the foot plough or the spade, had been the traditional way of life in the Highlands. The women usually went with the cattle to the *shielings*, the upland pastures in summer and the

Photo: Dennis Hardley

Highland drovers drove surplus cattle south in autumn to be sold, notably at Falkirk Tryst.

When landowners learned that sheep farmers from the south were willing to pay rents as much as three times higher, many of them cleared Highland people out of the glens to make room for big sheep farms. This happened in Strathnaver in Sutherland in 1819 when people were cleared from their homes,

Opposite: *A crofting community with some good pasture for cattle and sheep by the shores of Loch Kishorn.*

Above: *Crofter Donald MacDonald with his flock on the family croft, Isle of Skye.*

which were burned to prevent them returning, and moved to little strips of land called *crofts* on a rocky coast where they had to build their own houses and try to break up the ground to grow food. They were told that the sea would feed them if they would only take up fishing.

This was the origin of crofting settlements all along the north and west coasts of the Highlands, where the crofters were left with too little land,

having lost access to the common grazing and the shielings for their cattle. With population rising, more and more people became dependent on potatoes as their main source of food, grown even on land never cultivated before. When the crop failed, in the mid-1840s and in the early 1880s, people starved.

Clearance also caused many people to migrate to industrial towns in the south. Many others were caught up in the tide of emigration to a new life overseas, especially in Canada

A family of Highland cattle grazing in Glen Nevis, the traditional breed in the Highlands, formerly driven on foot to market in the south by drovers.

and the U.S., and later in Australia and New Zealand.

The popularity of deer stalking as a sport in the 1840s among English landowners and industrialists led them at first to pay high rents for shooting rights, and then to purchase Highland estates, especially in Ross-shire and Inverness-shire, and turn them into deer forests. The interest of Prince Albert, Queen Victoria's husband, in deer stalking and their purchase of Balmoral in 1846 helped to make Highland sporting holidays fashionable.

Horatio McCulloch's paintings of wild Highland scenery, such as *Misty Corries: Haunts of the Red Deer* (1847) and *Glencoe* (1864) contributed and the climax was probably reached with Edwin Landseer's painting of a stag which he called *Monarch of the Glen* (1851). Formerly the glens had been homes of the people.

By 1883 there were over 100 deer forests in the Highlands occupying over 2,000,000 acres. For the crofters this could mean clearance sometimes, loss of common grazings and deer eating their crops. When the Napier Commission travelled about the Highlands enquiring into crofting conditions in 1883,

Above: *High Bridge, built with three arches in 1736 over the River Spean, was once part of General Wade's military road to Inverness.*

they heard these complaints from crofters over and over again. The resulting Crofters Act (1886) made them secure in their crofts at low rents but failed to give them enough land.

A century later the Crofters Commission recognised that little had changed, calling crofting 'an anchor of population in an area of great scenic beauty…but with poor employment opportunities'.

Roads, Caledonian Canal and Railways

The first attempt to provide alternative work to stem the outflow of emigrants was made by the engineer, Thomas Telford in 1803. He suggested a great programme of public works - 900 miles of roads and 1000

bridges, harbours such as Wick, and the Caledonian Canal - which not only opened up the Highlands but taught new skills and provided work for three thousand men every year for a period of twenty years. The Canal (opened in 1822) is still in use today and so are many of the bridges, notably Mucomir Bridge in the Great Glen, Helmsdale far to the north, and Craigellachie (1814) in the north-east off the A95, its elegant arch spanning 150 feet, now the oldest iron bridge in Scotland.

Telford built roads where no-one had built a road before, to the west coast, for example, from Dingwall to Lochcarron, and outstandingly, from Inverness over great bridges and the Mound to Wick and finally Thurso on the north coast, a distance of 160 miles by 1819. His roads were for horses and coaches and carts and, some still, in Robert Southey's words, 'wind with the vale and win the long ascent'.

Modern road improvements have opened up the Highlands as never before, to cars, buses and lorries, notably the A9 from Perth to the north, which since 1974 has been made straighter, smoother and gentler in gradient, dual carriageway in places, by-passing villages such

as Aviemore and the town of Inverness, and crossing a former barrier, the Beauly Firth, by the splendid Kessock Bridge (opened 1982). Bridges have replaced west coast ferries at Ballachulish and Kylesku, for example, and controversially, at Kyle of Lochalsh for crossing to Skye. Built as a private venture, the tolls are high, about £5 per journey, compared with 40p on the Forth Road Bridge. Holidaymakers determined to sail 'over the sea to Skye' may still do so from Mallaig or Galtair near Glenelg.

Railways came late to the Highlands: Inverness via Nairn to Aviemore and the south (1863) but via Carrbridge not till 1898; Inverness to Wick and Thurso by 1874; Dingwall to Strome Ferry in 1870 but not reaching Kyle of Lochalsh (the Kyle Line for Skye) till 1897. The West Highland Line from Glasgow to Fort William opened in 1894 and reached Mallaig in 1911. All of these lines are still open and they are recommended as an easy and comfortable way to enjoy the ever changing scenery. 'The Jacobite' steam train from Fort

Opposite: Pleasure craft on the Caledonian Canal being raised from the level of Loch Ness through the five locks at Fort Augustus on their way south-west through the Great Glen.

Photo: Dennis Hardley

Above: *Helmsdale Bridge (1811) one of Thomas Telford's great stone bridges carrying the main road north to Wick.*

William to Mallaig and the Strathspey Steam Railway from Aviemore to Boat of Garten and beyond in summer attract railway enthusiasts to the Highlands.

Tartan and Highland Games

Highlanders have always liked check patterns. A man would wear a check *plaid* or 'great wrap' round his waist with the remainder thrown over his shoulder. Because the cloth was made locally, the patterns in an area tended to be similar, but all

the members of a clan would never be wearing exactly the same tartan.

When tartan and the kilt were banned after the 'Forty-five until 1782, Highlanders took to trousers, however unwillingly to start with, as their workaday garb, made of thick, plain material and that is what their descendants are wearing in late 19th century photographs.

The revival of tartan and the association of particular tartans with specific clans owes much to Sir Walter Scott and clan chiefs and their families wearing tartan for the visit of George IV to Edinburgh in 1822, the first visit by a Hanoverian monarch in over a century. He surprised many by appearing in Highland dress of Royal Stewart tartan.

The craze for tartan was fed by Messrs Wilson, weavers in Bannockburn, who invented many new patterns. There are clan tartans, hunting tartans, dress tartans and ancient tartans with paler colours. The variety is astonishing, best seen at Highland Games every summer in towns and villages all over the Highlands.

At Highland Games athletes compete, like heroes of old, in running and jumping, including distance races on the road or up the nearest hill. Others, the 'heavy men', compete in feats of strength - throwing the hammer, swinging it round but without moving their feet; throwing the weight over the bar; putting the shot; and tossing the caber, aiming for a complete turn straight ahead of the competitor.

Opposite: *Tormore Distillery, 12 miles east of Grantown-on-Spey, has been described as the most beautiful industrial structure in the Highlands. Whisky making is Scotland's toast to the world.* Photo: Dennis Hardley

Above: *Fly fishing by Loch Morlich in the Spey Valley, a popular holiday destination.*

Below: *A steam locomotive on the Strathspey Railway in summer.*

Going on at the same time are competitions in piping and Highland dancing.

The distinctly Highland team game is shinty (*camanachd* in Gaelic). Like hurling in Ireland it is a wilder form of hockey, since the stick can be raised above the shoulder. It is particularly strong in Badenoch where Newtonmore and Kingussie are great rivals.

Gaelic and the Mod

Gaelic, the Highland language, suffered when compulsory education was introduced in 1872, since children were taught

Opposite: Highland dancers during competition at the Highland games.
Photo: Dennis Hardley

Left: *A conversation at a Highland Gathering and two versions of Highland dress, one modest, the other splendid.*

Above: *Tossing the caber at the Highland games always exciting but very difficult.*

to read and write English and they were taught in English. The case for English was that Highland children would learn about the outside world and be able to communicate in it, since so many of them would have to leave home to make a living, but they were turning their backs on their native culture. Only in Sunday Schools did they learn to read their native Gaelic in the Gaelic Bible.

The National Mod, held annually somewhere in the

Highlands for over a hundred years is a great festival of Gaelic culture, poetry and singing, both solo and choral to maintain interest and standards through competition.

Within the last few years a popular Gaelic revival has begun (admittedly from a lower starting point than the case of the Welsh language).There has been a spontaneous boom in Gaelic playgroups for the youngest children and in Gaelic units in primary schools, 8000 adults actively learning Gaelic, besides courses taught in Gaelic in the Gaelic College Sabhal Mor Ostaig in Skye, a wide range of Gaelic radio and television programmes

offering opportunities for careers using Gaelic in the media and in teaching. There is also a cult following among the young for Gaelic folksong and bands such as Runrig.

Work in the Twentieth Century

Forestry became a large employer after the Second World War in people's home areas but after the planting stage was past, the numbers have declined.

Herring and white fish stocks have been seriously hit due to overfishing, as have stocks of mackerel formerly caught out of Ullapool. Fish farming is the new growth activity, trout inland and salmon in the long sea lochs, and feeding them and processing - cleaning, smoking and packaging - are important new occupations, while local fisherman tend to concentrate now on catching lobsters and shellfish for the luxury market.

Although not employing many workers, Highland distilleries carry on traditional whisky-making, most producing malt whisky. The name is from Gaelic

Opposite: Fishermen drawing in their salmon nets from the tidal Kyle of Sutherland at Bonar Bridge, its modern bowstring arch bridge (1973) on the left.
Photo: Dennis Hardley

Photo: Dennis Hardley

Above: *Dramatic sea cliffs at Duncansby Head near John o' Groats in Caithness.*

uisge beatha 'the water of life' and the ingredients are pure Highland water, malted barley, yeast and a hint of peat-smoke. Distilled in copper 'pot stills', it matures in oak casks for 3 years before it can be called 'Scotch' and far longer for single malts.

Scotch whisky, 96% of which is blended, requiring many different malts, is a high value product, heavily taxed by the Exchequer but which makes a huge contribution to exports - six times as much is exported than is consumed in Great Britain.

Hydro-electric schemes between 1945 and 1975 to use the Highlands' ample water supplies to produce electricity efficiently and cleanly have brought light and power to

Highland homes and allowed industries to set up anywhere.

The number of large industrial employers in the Highlands is not high, however, paper-making at Corpach for example, and aluminium smelting in Lochaber, whereas the building of oil production platforms at Nigg and Ardersier kept large numbers of skilled workers in employment for a number of years.

Only one person out of every twenty-five in Scotland lives in the Highlands. Population actually increased in the Highlands between 1971 and 1981 by 12.5% but most of the increase has taken place in towns, especially in the biggest

town, Inverness. 'Capital of the Highlands', headquarters of Highlands and Islands Enterprise, headquarters of Highland Council who are employers of large numbers of officials, carers and teachers, Inverness also contains hospitals, government agencies and tourist offices which all provide services of some kind.

Many people cater for tourists, in hotels and 'bed and breakfasts', from bus drivers to garage mechanics, rangers to ski instructors, artists and craftspeople to people who work in shops, the heritage industry

Opposite: Ullapool on Loch Broom is a busy fishing port and ferry terminal for the Isle of Lewis in the Outer Hebrides.

Photo: Dennis Hardley

and information centres, but not all of these are all year round occupations.

Thanks to modern digital communications, new firms have proved that it is possible to conduct business from the Highlands and serve customers all over the world.

Similar equipment makes distance learning possible and will link 11 technical colleges in an exciting new university for the Highlands and Islands.

The Highlands for Holidays
Many people come just to enjoy the scenery. The weather they find relatively mild as a rule, thanks to the closeness of the sea in the long sea lochs and the Gulf Stream, which encouraged

Above: *Inverness, administrative centre and the largest town in the Highlands, has the River Ness flowing through it, its banks lined with churches and crossed by many bridges.*

Osgood MacKenzie to create a wonderful sub-tropical garden at Inverewe. Rainfall, heaviest in the leeward rainshadow of the mountains of the west can reach 80 inches a year, but only about 28 inches at Inverness in the east. It gives greenness to the landscape, power to the water-falls and mountain streams, and the light after rain adds sparkle and brightness to the views.

Climbers and hillwalkers seeking the higher summits and high level cross-country skiers are coming to the Highlands in increasing numbers. Over half a million of them came from

Photo: A D Cameron

Ancient Caledonian Forest in the Glenmore Forest Reserve, Cairngorms.

Britain in 1995 and they stayed 11 days each on the average. It is well worth noting that their contribution to the Highland economy, in terms of the amount they spent and the number of jobs they created, is now greater than that made by the traditional sportsmen who come for deer-stalking and grouse shooting.

The Cairngorms and the Nevis Range have developed most for skiers, thanks to their steep north-facing corries to hold the windblown snow, and investment in access roads, chairlifts in the Cairngorms and gondola cable cars at Aonach Mor in the Nevis Range.

These are the areas which attract mountaineers and hillwalkers too, along with Glencoe and Skye, and followed by Kintail and Torridon.

At lower levels Forest Enterprise and some estates provide interesting forest trails for walkers and mountain bikers, another fast growing outdoor activity. Forest Enterprise in Glenmore and the Royal Society for the Protection of Birds in Abernethy Forest are taking steps to encourage the natural regeneration of Scots pine, the native woodland of the Highlands.

Besides Abernethy the RSPB has several Highland bird reserves from Glenborrodale in the south-west to the Insh Marshes near Kingussie, the Culbin Sands on the Moray Firth and Forsinard in the Flow Country. The National Trust for Scotland owns land of outstanding beauty, Glencoe for example, the Five Sisters of Kintail, and the mountains of Torridon, and the Scottish Wildlife Trust and the Woodland Trust are both active in conservation in the Highlands.

The north-west Highlands has often been described as 'the last great wilderness'. Since wilderness can sometimes be made by man, 'wildness' is perhaps a better word, as John Muir, the great Scottish campaigner for National Parks in America, taught. 'Do something for wildness', he urged, 'and make the mountains glad'.

Acting on this advice the John Muir Trust has purchased estates in Skye to keep the Cuillins wild and open and unspoilt, while co-operating closely with local people who are making a living in the area. The north-west too is precious, full of secret, silent places, pleasing to the eye and refreshing to the spirit.